Carmen Disruption

Olivier-Award winner Simon Stephens is one of the most prolific contemporary playwrights and his work is produced across the world. The author of more than twenty stage plays, including *Punk Rock*, *Port*, *Three Kingdoms* and *Pornography*, as well as the celebrated adaptation of *The Curious Incident of the Dog in the Night-Time*, he is a former tutor on the Royal Court Young Writers Programme. Awards include the Pearson Award for Best New Play, 2001, for *Port*; Olivier Award for Best New Play for *On the Shore of the Wide World*, 2005; and Best Foreign Playwright, as voted by German critics in Theater Heute's annual poll, 2007.

T0286339

Works by Simon Stephens published by Bloomsbury Methuen Drama

Plays

Birdland
Blindsided
The Cherry Orchard (*English-language version*)
Christmas
Country Music
The Curious Incident of the Dog in the Night-Time (*adaptation*)
A Doll's House (*English-language version*)
Harper Regan
Herons
Morning
Motortown
On the Shore of the Wide World
One Minute
Pornography (*also in the Student Edition series*)
Port
Punk Rock
Sea Wall
A Thousand Stars Explode in the Sky
(*with David Eldridge and Robert Holman*)
Three Kingdoms
The Trial of Ubu
Wastwater *and* T5

Collected works

STEPHENS PLAYS: 1
(Bluebird, Christmas, Herons, Port)

STEPHENS PLAYS: 2
(One Minute, Country Music, Motortown, Porngraphy, Sea Wall)

STEPHENS PLAYS: 3
(Harper Regan, Punk Rock, Marine Parade and
On the Shore of the Wide World)

Simon Stephens

Carmen Disruption

Bloomsbury Methuen Drama
An imprint of Bloomsbury Publishing Plc

B L O O M S B U R Y
LONDON · NEW DELHI · NEW YORK · SYDNEY

Bloomsbury Methuen Drama
An imprint of Bloomsbury Publishing Plc

Imprint previously known as Methuen Drama

50 Bedford Square	1385 Broadway
London	New York
WC1B 3DP	NY 10018
UK	USA

www.bloomsbury.com

**BLOOMSBURY and the Diana logo are registered
trademarks of Bloomsbury Publishing Plc**

© Simon Stephens, 2015

Simon Stephens has asserted his right under the Copyright, Designs
and Patents Act, 1988, to be identified as author of this work.

This version of the text went to print before the end of rehearsals
and may differ slightly from the version performed.

All rights whatsoever in this play are strictly reserved and application
for performance, etc. should be made before rehearsals begin to
Casarotto Ramsay & Associates Ltd, Waverley House, 7–12 Noel Street,
London W1F 8GQ. Mail to: agents@casarotto.co.uk. No performance
may be given unless a licence has been obtained.

No rights in incidental music or songs contained in the work are hereby
granted and performance rights for any performance/presentation
whatsoever must be obtained from the respective copyright owners.

British Library Cataloguing-in-Publication Data
A catalogue record for this book is available from the British Library.

ISBN: PB: 978-1-4742-5160-0
ePub: 978-1-4742-5162-4
ePDF: 978-1-4742-5161-7

Library of Congress Cataloging-in-Publication Data
A catalog record for this book is available from the Library of Congress.

Typeset by Mark Heslington Ltd, Scarborough, North Yorkshire
Printed and bound in Great Britain

Carmen Disruption

Carmen Disruption was first performed at the Deutsche
Schauspielhaus, Hamburg, on 15 March 2014, featuring the
following cast and creative team:

Carmen	Christoph Luser
The Singer	Rinat Shaham
Don José	Julia Wieninger
Escamillo	Samuel White
Micaëla	Anne Müller

Director	Sebastian Nübling
Designer	Dominic Huber
Costume designer	Amit Epstein
Composer	Lars Wittershagen
Lighting designer	Rebecca Dahnke
Dramaturg	Sybille Meier

The play received its UK premiere at the Almeida Theatre,
London, on 10 April 2015, with the following cast and
creative team:

The Singer	Sharon Small
Carmen	Jack Farthing
Don José	Noma Dumezweni
Escamillo	John Light
Micaëla	Katie West
Chorus	Viktoria Vizin
Ensemble/Cellist	Jamie Cameron
Ensemble/Cellist	Harry Napier

Direction	Michael Longhurst
Design	Lizzie Clachan
Composition and Musical Direction	Simon Slater
Movement Direction	Imogen Knight
Light	Jack Knowles
Sound	Carolyn Downing

Casting	Anne McNulty CDG and Sarah Playfair
Dramaturg	Pia Furtado
Assistant Direction	Jude Christian
Costume Supervision	Jemima Penny
Assistant Musical Direction	Neil Macdonald
Casting Assistant	Ruth O'Dowd

Characters

The Singer, *female – thirties*
Micaëla, *female – late teens*
Don José, *female – fifties*
Carmen, *male – twenties*
Escamillo, *male – thirties*
Chorus

This play takes its structure from the 1875 opera Carmen by Georges Bizet.

It was written at the provocation of my friend and colleague Sebastian Nübling.

It is informed by lengthy conversations with the mezzo-soprano Rinat Shaham. I am completely indebted to her for her generosity and insight and openness.

The Singer   A rank of taxis waits outside the opera house.

Three women leave the offices in the beautiful old building across the square from where I'm standing. They're smoking cigarettes and they link their arms together and they're singing. I can't hear the song that they're singing.

Two policemen stand on the corner of the square and watch the women. They try to say goodnight to them but the girls just start giggling. The policemen don't mind. They're used to this kind of thing.

A young girl comes into the square from the direction of the river. She's trying to make a phone call to her father. She can't get through. She leaves a message.

A tired looking man in a suit climbs into the back of a taxi and the driver, I think she's a woman, turns her engine on and puts the car into gear and slides away.

A boy drinks a beer by the side of the opera. I know that I should go and hold his hand. Ask him to buy a beer for me. I don't. I stand. Still as a stone.

Chorus   We thrust hands deep into our pockets.
We sing sweet little songs to ourselves.
We take care not to bump into each other.
We pop chocolates under our tongues.
We save our receipts for our records.
We hook shopping bags over our arms.
We drink cold beer in the afternoon.
We wear sunglasses in the grey light.

The Singer   I am trying very hard to keep this as simple and as clear as I can.

I have a voice in my head. It's a voice that tells me everything I should do.

Micaëla   I have decided now that it is my responsibility to remember everything that has ever happened to me. I realise nobody else can do this but me.

I have started losing all sense of my past.
Our memories are imagined. We remember the things we
wished were true even though we know they're not.
And if that's the case then anything could be true.
Really anything.

These are some of the things that happened to me today.
I had three pancakes for breakfast.
I washed my hair.
I found a song that my brother used to play in his bedroom
on YouTube and played it very loud.
I saw a boy not much older than me crash his motorbike into
the wall of a bridge and fly fifteen feet in the air and land on
his head and stop moving.
I remembered Alexander and cried and cried.
I walked the whole length of the town where I live because I
knew I had no money for the train fare.
My grandmother was buried, this morning, back in the town
where I was born and I couldn't go because of my work and
because I had no money and I was going to call my dad and
ask him to bring me home in time for the funeral but I didn't.
I stood at the side of the river and for a long time wondered
how cold the water would have been in real life and if I was
wearing all my clothes I wondered how long it would
actually take me to drown.
I wondered what it would feel like to drown.
I contemplated a future without a degree.
I realised I would do anything to get him to come back to me.

We're gonna kill
The California girls
We're gonna fire the exploding load in the milkmaid
maiden head
We're gonna find the meaning
Of feeling good
And we're gonna stay there as long as we think we should
Mystery train
To Your Brain

Expressway
To Your skull

Alexander called me.
Nine forty-two this morning.
Introduced himself as Professor Schmidt.
I was speechless.
Really?
He asked me: Can I get my essay to the departmental office
by five?
I couldn't believe he honestly asked me that question.
I told him I'd emailed it to him.
He said me, 'The office need a hard copy, Micaëla.'
I told him to fucking print the fucking thing out.
He went quiet.
What? What have you gone all quiet for?
I need to sign it in.
I need to hand it over and sign the submission document.
I told him to forge my signature.
I told him he definitely knew what my signature looked like.
I told him I was tired because I was up until half three.
I asked him if he wanted to know what I'd been doing.

The Singer   It tells me what to do as the plane taxis gently
towards the terminal.

It tells me when to stand up from my seat and how long to
wait before everybody else has got down from the plane. It
tells me where the best place to wait for my luggage is. I've
two cases. One full of work clothes and medicine. One full of
the things that I need to just stay alive.

Carmen   I catch myself in the mirror as I'm heading into
the kitchen to get some coffee from the stove and I take
myself by surprise because I look fucking amazing.

I put a small bottle of lube in the side pocket of my satchel
and two packets of condoms, one normal size and one extra
large. I've got a packet of Viagra in my wallet and some wet
wipes and some Listerine and my deodorant. A small bottle
of poppers. My mobile phone.

In my carriage on the subway into the Old Town I'm completely on my own. I hang by the handrails and stare into my reflection. My face is distended by the curve of the window. I look like I've got a remarkably long head. I don't in real life. My head is kind of beautifully proportioned.

A man gets on just as I'm getting off. He moves to one side to let me pass. I smile a thank you at him and it melts his heart.

As the train pulls away it screams and it smells like burning.

I take three steps at a time as I'm climbing out of the subway. I feel alert. I feel alive. I come out into the Old Town by the shops beneath the cathedral and there's a woman there, staring at me. She's about forty years old. Thick black curly hair and eyes like coal. She can't stop looking at me. I can't say I blame her.

I flick the wheel on my lighter and watch the flame catch the end of my cigarette and it's like everybody starts walking in slow motion to stare.

I need a shirt.

There's a girl behind the counter at Hugo Boss with eyes like they're made out of wood. She barely talks to me. She doesn't smile. The speed with which the card machine accepts my transaction is breathtaking even to me.

I ask her. Can I wear it now? Can I put it on here?

It sits under my jacket which is old and leather and smells of the fifties and I've got a Pierre Cardin scarf from the seventies which is made out of pure silk and the combination is astonishing. I'm giving myself an erection.

The Singer   It tells me where to get my sleeping pills and where to get my energy drink and where to get new earplugs and where to get a new bra and where to get some tin foil and where to get some masking tape to stick my tin foil to the window.

It tells me not to worry that I can't afford these things. Not now. Not really.

Don José   You'll be surprised. When you see me you won't recognise me. Nobody does. Nobody thinks I'm actually doing this for real. Nobody believes this is actually a real thing and you won't either.

I'll be thinking about you all the time.

You'll be getting yourself ready and probably you'll be having second thoughts because you always have second thoughts and even when you were a little boy, you used to have second thoughts and be afraid of things and that's natural and normal and you need to know that it's natural and normal but I promise you, you will be fine and you will be safe and I would never, ever, do anything to hurt you.

I'll have been preparing myself for weeks and weeks. I'll have re-read your email a million times. Your name comes into my inbox and it's like a bomb goes off in the pit of my stomach. My son.

And when I get up and I stumble for a piss and I brush my teeth and I have a shower and I make my toast and I boil my eggs and I make my coffee and I drink my coffee and I head out of my door and climb into my car I will only really be thinking of you.

I know exactly how my working day will start because my working day always starts in the same way. I know exactly what my first fares will be like. I know how sleepy they will be. I know how urgent their conversations on their mobile phones will be. I know this urgency will last until half way through the morning.

I know there will be a moment at around half past ten in that morning that I'll find myself stopping. There's a little quiet square where we all go and have a coffee and a break and a chat and a think and just by there, there is a university or a college or something. I like to watch the students there.

They leave me uplifted. They give me hope. I'll spend some time watching them. And when I do I will notice that one of them will look like you. There is always one of them who looks like you and today will be no different.

He'll have the same hair as I remember you having. He'll move in the same way and he'll talk to his friends in the same way. They'll all be talking so quickly and with such excitement that I'll want to go over and just join in their conversation. I won't. Don't worry. Honestly. I really won't.

The Singer   In the past six months I've lived in three different cities.

I've stayed at home on precisely five nights.

On three of those nights I was on my own.

I get to the place where the lady on Airbnb told me I could collect the keys for the apartment and I get to the apartment and everything is fine and I get the keys so that's all great and everything is falling nicely into place. I get into the apartment. There's a garden. I can't believe there's a garden. I can't believe I can breathe.

I go into the room where I'm going to sleep.

I have two hours. I sleep.

Micaëla   Alexander left me because my friend offered to suck his cock at a party we all went to and she's quite experienced at that kind of thing. She knew these tricks with her tongue where she twists her hand one way and licks her tongue the other and after that he didn't really stand much of a chance did he? I can't remember if he stayed in the party for a long time afterwards or not.

I was thinking about exactly this point when I decided to wash my hair in the shower. I like the feeling of washing my hair normally. Normally the shampoo makes me feel better for reasons that I don't understand. What does all that water have to do with the things that we want? That's what I couldn't understand as I dried myself with a towel that was more threadbare than I remembered it being and a little bit damp because I hadn't hung it up to dry after I last used it. What do all those hair follicles have to do with the feeling of what it is to be lonely? Or the horror of knowing that right now my father's mother is being buried and I can't be there for him because I have to deliver my essay and I have no money to get home.

My essay is an essay about an English novelist from the last century. It's very, very bad. It might be the worst essay that I've ever written. It might actually be the worst essay that anybody has ever written.

Alexander left me because I never stopped crying after we had sex. I'd want to hold on to him tightly. I'd want him to hold my hand for ever and keep his arm around me even when we went to cafes or the cinema. After a while it drove him insane.

Do you think it's possible to have sex with somebody without actually touching them?

On the side of the petrol station at the corner of my street somebody has painted the words: 'Shadows we are. And like Shadows we depart.'

Don José   At about half past ten I'll get a text from a man I've driven a few times now. He's a man I'm in debt to for reasons that I will never tell you.
It's very simple.
There's a job he wants me to do.
It's a driving job. It's easy. After I do this job my debt to him will be paid. I won't have a choice.

As if this is the kind of thing that happens in real life. Today. Of all days.

I can't. Not today. I'm meant to be seeing my son today.

I could send a text back to this 'man who I am in some way indebted to'. I could refuse to do his work for him. I could go and meet him. I could tell him to his face. I could kick his fucking teeth in. He'll look at me and he can sense it. I could kick your teeth into the back of your throat. You'd be picking them out for weeks, handsome. Should have seen me when I was a girl. If you'd seen me then. Or been to the places I went to. Or met some of the people I met.

After next Wednesday it will have been seven years since I've spoken to either you or your sister and eight years since I left you. I am happy to take responsibility for that. I know it's my fault.

Micaëla   Alexander left me because after my grandmother died I talked for hours about death.

I talked to him about how shit it was and how painful it was and how much pain she was in and how awful it was that it was just inevitable. It's that we know, actually. That's the sickest cruellest joke that God ever played. Let us know that we'll die but not let us know when or how or what happens afterwards or give us any ability to stop the thing at all.

That is just fucking horrible.

I mean is that just me? It might just be me.

I do believe in God. A lot of people my age don't believe in God anymore but I do.

I believe in God. I believe in churches. I believe in temples. I believe in mosques. I believe in synagogues. There's a temple at the end of my street actually. It's a Sikh temple. Every New Year's Eve the community light fireworks into the sky. Some of the fireworks are great. Some are a bit shit. The small shit fireworks catch on the trees because they haven't got the energy to get any higher. They land there. They look like lanterns bursting loud and crashing into the sky.

I walked past the American car wash. The music from the stereos there boomed out throughout the street and made it vibrate. It was some trashy fucking horrible American pop song. Some girl singing about some guy who'd treated her badly but she was going to be fine. Stupid cunt.

I walked past the cafes on the edge of the financial district. I thought I needed to put my sunglasses on. Right at that second in a city hundreds of miles away everyone was arriving at my grandmother's funeral. Probably a lot of them will be wearing sunglasses too.

I wonder how much six feet of solid earth weighs.

My grandmother wasn't on Facebook. I told her to go on Facebook but she didn't. I told her to go on Twitter but she didn't. If she'd gone on Facebook or gone on Twitter she would still have been alive in a way. I called her mobile phone six times after she died just to hear her voicemail and then her batteries ran out.

The Singer   I wake up. I shower. I try to figure out the exact shape of the place.

The woman who owns the place has left all her photographs on the wall of her and her friends and – Are they her children? Does she have children? Where are they? Where are her children? If she's just left her place? After a while I think about her bed. I have the strongest sensation that she slept in my bed the night before I arrived. The shape on the pillow where her head must have lay. I can't help feeling that I've been here before. Have I been here before?

I do what I always do. I take the pictures off the wall. I put them in a drawer. I take some scarves out of my bag. I drape them over her things. I check the WiFi signal. It has three bars. It's good. The password works just fine. 'Habanera.'

Carmen   I want a drink.

There's a bar that I know in the basement of a building that used to be a fur factory. I want to show my new shirt off. I've got three hours till my date. It's one thirty in the afternoon. I want to drink a gin and tonic.

Rudi always has the TVs on. No matter what time it is. You come into his bar and almost straightaway you lose any sense of what time it is outside. He's got three different films running at the same time and Daft Punk playing on his Bose speakers.

Touch.
Sweet Touch.
You almost convinced me I'm real.

Three black guys with white condoms and huge cocks are fucking a white teenager. His eyes have the dead, dry look that you can only really get with Ketamine. Even without the sound on, even with the music in the bar as loud as it is I can tell that the film is Italian. This kind of racial politics is part of their scene. Porno reveals more about a country than anything else nowadays.

Rudi lets me smoke in the bar. He lights my cigarette without me having to ask him to. The flame sits in the air.

I like this place. I feel very at home here. I like that it exists in every city. And that wherever I am, in any country in the whole wide world there is always a Rudi's and I can always find it and I always, always, always feel at home.

This guy comes over. He calls himself Jacques. He spells it in the French style. He buys me a second gin and tonic. He starts talking to me.

He looks like Eddie Constantine in *Alphaville* but when he opens his mouth I swear to you, I am not shitting you, he says the most boring fucking tedious horrible nonsense that I think any human has ever said about anything.

He talks to me straight for fifty-eight minutes without pausing once. Even for breath. He talks to me mainly about his work. I feel like telling him to shut the fuck up, I'm trying to watch a movie here, but I don't. I'm well raised in that sense.

'And my boss emails me. Get this. Right. I'm meant to be on a training day. That's why I'm here. Right. He emails me. Which is clever. Coz, right, I could refuse to answer a phone call. I could pretend I had my phone on silent. But I can't

exactly ignore his email can I? Can I though? I can't. No.
Because they keep a record of it on the company server.
They can tell exactly when you've accessed your account
even to glance at it. They say that it's to incentivise us. They
tell us it's a motivational tactic. I watched a fucking
PowerPoint they did about it in a conference they all invited
us to. They monitor our performance and they offer regular
consultations with the human resources office. So they know.
You know? They know what we're looking at and what we're
not looking at. He says to me. Can I file the report by the
end of the day? I say to him. I'm on a training day. I can't file
the report. Because that's what this is to me. This is a
training day.'

He tells me about his children. Tells me about his wife and
how very much he loves her and he says it as though like
that is something that nobody has ever told me before. He
tells me he's never done this before. He's never been to a
place like this before. I finish my drink. Bum a packet of
matches from Rudi. I've got to leave. I'm sorry. There's
somebody I need to see.

The Singer   What's she like this woman? Whose head lay
on my pillow? Whose clothes hang in my closet? I look at her
clothes. I take down her clothes. I try them on. I enjoy the
feeling of her clothes against my skin. I cry for a little bit but
only a little bit and then stop.

Carmen   It's warm.
It's getting warmer.
Somewhere there's a fire. I can smell it.
It is as though
Suddenly
Spring has arrived

The Singer   I dream about the voice in my head. I always
dream about the voice in my head. Sometimes it's a man's
voice but mostly it's a woman's voice. Mostly it's the woman
whose story I tell. I always dream about her on the first day.
More precisely I dream about her clothes.

I have worn her clothes a hundred times. I've worn her clothes in a hundred cities. I have said the things that she says. I have moved my hands in exactly the way that she moves her hands. When I put on this corset where does the stitching end? Where does she start? Where do I end?

Don José   At about eleven o'clock I will stop my car at a pedestrian crossing. I will watch the two crowds of strangers gathered on either side of the street to move towards one another at a given signal. They have never met. They will never meet. They get on their marks. They get set.

One of them stops as she's crossing the road. She looks me right in the eye. A woman with thick curly black hair. She stands there as she's crossing the road in front of me and she stares.

Carmen   The way he looks at me, when he sees me. His eyes light up like a fucking child on Christmas Day. He's got a Parmigiani Fleurier watch on his wrist, a twinkle in his eye and a hard on the size of the Empire State Building. He gave my name to the staff at the club lounge of the hotel. They didn't even bat an eye.

He asks me if my name's really Carmen. I ask him if I look like a liar.

He asks me how I like the wine. He asks me how I like the bar. He asks me how I like this street. He asks me how I like this town. He tells me about something that happened here and I can't really concentrate but it seems that a long time ago, like before I was born, something horrible happened here like some children were killed here or some fucking shit. I zone out and concentrate on the feeling of my new shirt and take out my Viagra and pop it in my mouth right in front of him and look him right in the eye.

When I come it's like a fucking bullet from a gun. It's hard and its straight and it's hot and its fast and you feel it and sometimes I think the only fair thing to do is to warn people. To let them know.

There is a fake log fire in one corner of his suite. It's gas powered. He shows me how it turns on and off.

His bed is fucking huge. The room smells of his cologne. It's musky. He tells me he's going to take a shower and that I should be ready for him when he gets back.

I fold my clothes immaculately. Have a good smell of my shirt. I love the way new shirts smell. I lie on top of the bed waiting for him like a little girl in a porno film. Some fucking babysitter or something.

He comes back. He unwraps the hotel towel. His cock is bigger than some guys and smaller than others. Which in the end is how cocks tend to be. He tells me he doesn't do kissing. He asks me if that's okay. I tell him whatever turns you on, baby-face.

He smiles at me. Turns me over.

He tells me that he only ever rides bareback. He tells me he'll pay me an extra three hundred euros. He promises to cum on my face. He tells me he never uses lubricant because he doesn't trust the chemicals. He uses four fingers to force open my rectum. It really fucking hurts. I ask him if I can get my poppers and he punches the side of my face.

People get. They do these things. Don't judge him. Don't fucking. Don't. Don't judge him. It's just something that sometimes people do.

He doesn't pull out. I can feel it. He shudders. Grows hot. Roars a little bit. Shakes.

For a few seconds I can't speak to him.

What the fuck do you think you're doing? You can suck it out of my fucking arse. I'll swear at who the fuck I want, you fucking piece of shit. You fucking faggot. You promised me.

He picks up the phone to call security. I knock it out of his hand.

You can pay me now. Five hundred extra. You can't do that. You can't do what you did to me.

I'm surprised by how quickly he falls when I hit him. He crumples like he's made out of sticks.

He doesn't make a noise.

He lies there like he's pretending. Like he's acting out what you're meant to do when a rent boy punches you in the side of your head. In the thick warm carpet of his hotel suite.

I kick him in his ribs with my bare feet which kind of hurts but kind of doesn't. I kick him in the side of his arm. I stamp my foot on his neck. I kick the side of his head. His skin breaks by his cheekbone so that blood spits out onto the carpet and catches between my toes. I hear the break of teeth under my feet. He's crying and kind of half screaming so I know he's not dead. It feels fucking fantastic.

I get dressed. I clean the blood off my toes before I put my socks on. I wonder if I've broken my middle toe on my right foot. I try wriggling it. It'll be fine. I look for his wallet. He left it on the table of his room. I take out nine hundred euros in cash. He's whimpering a bit. I drop the wallet on the floor. I check myself in the mirror before I leave.

I see if I can hold my hand still. Steady.

I walk out of the hotel. Wink at the girl on reception. Smile at the man on the door. Thank him when he holds it open for me.

Chorus   We see doctors taking photographs.
We see pornography on your phone.
We see yellow colours everywhere.
We see children playing in the street.
We see women wearing leather coats.
We see dogs straining on their leads.
We see words scratched into the walls.
We see faces shining in the glass.

The Singer   I go for a walk. I like walking in cities. I like all the confusion and the chaos and the amazing way people move around one another without ever touching one another.

There's something about this city that is stranger than others. There's something about this city that makes me think it isn't real. There's something about the city that makes it look like a stage set. There's something about the city that makes it feel like an opera.

I keep thinking there's somebody behind me. There isn't. I check.

Don José   Before I meet you I'll do what he asked me to do.

I'll go to the train station despite the wretched fucking traffic. I'll take a train eight miles east to the airport. Leave the airport station. Find my way to the shuttle bus to the long-stay car park. I'll go to the car park. I'll find the red Renault that is parked in exactly the place that he told me it would be, and on the front left tyre there'll be a key that I'll find straight away. It will be so obvious from a distance that I'll be astonished nobody else will have taken the car before me. I'll open the car. I'll start the engine. I'll leave. I'll pay the toll. It'll be a lot cheaper than I expect it to be and I'll figure out how long the car has been parked there and that will take me by surprise. I'll follow the directions on the satellite navigator. I'll think about you. That will put my mind at rest.

I'll drive the car in the direction of what the sat nav calls 'home' and try not to remember where I'm going or any of the people that I see on the way there. I'll concentrate on the driving. I'll tell myself over and over again, 'You don't have any choice, Don José. You don't have any choice. This is what you promised him you would do.' As I drive it will become clear to me that the place that is recorded as 'home' on the sat nav is a storage depot three miles south of the city. I'll relax when I figure this out because I know that place well. I know a good way of getting back to the city from here. I'll pass two police cars but they won't pay the slightest bit of attention to me.

I'll try not to think about what's in the boot.

I'll try not to think about the smell. I'll try not to think about the stain on the back seat.

I'll park the car. I'll leave the depot. I'll walk to the bus stop. My debt will be paid. I'll catch a bus back into town.

As I'm crossing from the bus stop at the station to where I parked my car, a boy, a young boy in a beautiful shirt will walk right into me. He won't be looking where he's going. He won't apologise or look me in the eye.

The Singer   I wanted to be an actor.
I only did the singing because I couldn't get a place in acting school.
That's the truth. Actually.
That is actually the truth.
And then I decided to stay.
I like the way it makes me feel.
I like the way it makes my belly feel.
I like how it feels in my neck.

Carmen   I need to go somewhere. I need to get out of here. I need to think about where I'm going to go.

Mum. Mum, it's me. It's Carmen. Can I come and see you? Can I come and see you, Mum? I'm coming to see you.

On the train the woman in front of me has her bag right in front of her. I can't move my feet. I say to her. I can't move my fucking feet. Can you move your bag? Do you think? For one second. I'm trying to sit here. I'm trying to sit still here. I only want to breathe. All these fucking people with their stupid bags and their stupid faces. My toes hurt. My fist hurts. If I could I'd stand the whole journey. When I move, my arse feels like it's tearing in half.

Some people are just rude.

Don't ignore me. Don't fucking ignore me. You think you can turn your back on me. You think you can get away without loving me? Have you seen my shirt? Have you seen my fucking hair? Do you really think you can look at a man with hair like this and not break your heart into a million pieces. Because you try that. You try it and I will tear you in two.

I could get off the train. I could pull the alarm cord of the train. I could talk to the woman in front of me with the bag. I could tell her what happened to me this afternoon. I could call the police. I could tell them what I did. I could tell my mum. I could write to the paper. I could sit here and just cry. Let the tears fall down my face. I could change seats and go and sit with the man in the Paul Smith suit who is sitting on his own two-thirds of the way down the corridor. I could sing. I could open up my throat and sing as loud and as hard as I can.

I get out of the train at my mother's station and walk towards her house without even thinking.

I walk up to the edge of the road that leads to her street. There's a car coming. I step into the road. It accelerates. I don't stop. It swerves past me. It swerves.

The Singer   At the coffee break on the first day one of the ensemble I think, one of the cigarette girls I think or one of the orchestra it might have been but anyway somebody asks me where the last job I played was and who was the last director I worked with and I can't remember. I can't. I can't. I'm so sorry. It's so embarrassing. I had to look it up on my phone.

Sometimes I find conversation difficult.
When I could be singing. I find myself feeling like I should sing at somebody rather than just –

If I'm really telling you the truth, the only time I ever feel real anymore is when I'm her.

A traveller trapped by her tarot cards.
A rebel restricted by fate.
A lover unable to move any more.
Did you ever get a day like that?

Escamillo   I was never like this. You need to understand that.

If you'd told me at school that this is what would happen to me, if you'd told me at school that before the age of forty I would be staying in a hotel room like this in a city like this with a suit like that draped over the back of a chair like that, with that much money in a wallet made of leather that soft, with that calibre of mineral water bottle sitting on the table at the edge of my bed, well, I don't think I would have believed you at all.

And yet.

Here we are.

It takes me twenty seconds to remember which city I'm in. It always takes me twenty seconds to remember which city I'm in. I've stayed in twelve hotels in ten different cities in the past three months. After a while they start to blur into one another. Even back here. Even in this place. It's been so long.

The light falling through the curtains feels the same in every one. The linen on the duvet cover feels the same. The atmosphere of the air conditioning machine feels the same. The quietness of the soundproofing has the same effect.

I always dream the same type of dreams in these places. I dream the kind of dreams that make me feel like I will never die.

Three things. Before you check in to any hotel have a walk around the neighbourhood for at least fifteen minutes, regardless of what time you arrive and regardless of how many times you've been to this city before. Then once you're in the room spend fifteen minutes on Streetview. It is imperative that you know exactly where you are. So that when those twenty seconds pass, you can go. Just go.

If you're staying in a country that is very alien to the country you live in then make the fuck sure you buy yourself enough

Marlboro Gold or Diet Coke or Pringles or Snickers bars to sustain the duration of your stay. It is only through the things that you buy that you can ever feel at home any more.

And never, ever stay anywhere without a gym. And a steam room. And a sauna. And a pool.

I do forty five minutes on the Cybex rowing machine. Press forty kilogrammes for twenty minutes before steaming, ice bath, sauna and shower. Black Peppercorn Body Wash. Shower at thirty-two degrees. When you open up your pores then you open up your neurones. The connections are sharper. The synapses are more alert. Fact.

This morning I'll wear my Thomas Pink white shirt. No tie. Cashmere socks. I always wear cashmere on a day like today.

I take my breakfast overlooking the river. Grapefruit. Blackberries. Coffee.

For a moment I even forget which country I'm in. In spite of everything. For a moment I forget if I've been here before.

Because the shops are all the same and the roads are all the same and the airports are the same and the hotels are the same and the drinks are all the same and the food is all the same and the music is the same and the cars are all the same and the films are all the same and the football is the same and the television is the same. Everybody has lost all real sense of landscape. All natural resources are commoditised and transportable. The only way we continue nowadays is by selling the selling of the selling of the selling of every last thing that we sell. And you can do that from anywhere.

It's only in Russia that I've not felt that. I fucking hate Russia. They have shit chocolate in Russia. They have shit cigarettes. I never understood a single word anybody said to me there.

I have been here before though. This is the city I was born in.

I walk from the hotel. The feeling of my clothes against my skin makes me feel lighter than I've ever felt. I drink a two-litre bottle of mineral water on my way.
I start to remember exactly where I am. It starts to make me feel in some small way sad. There are people who still live here.

The sky is a shade of blue that I don't think I've ever seen in my whole life.

There is a breeze that is as light as silk.

I've got a week. If I'm lucky.

Two months ago I borrowed 400 million US dollars from pension funds based in Hamburg and Oslo.

I invested 250 million dollars invested in the manufacture of aluminium in China and of fertiliser for beef cultivation. Over the next five years the acceleration of demand for tinned beef amongst the burgeoning middle classes of China will blow your fucking mind. That's clear. The increase in aluminium for tins to contain the beef and for fertiliser to cultivate the livestock will be exponential.

I invested a further 150 million dollars in the distribution of rice as a cheap staple in the event of the economy moving the other way. Look into my eyes. I can see the future. There are things that I know to my core will happen here.

What I hadn't anticipated was –
What I hadn't anticipated was –
What I hadn't anticipated was –

There is nothing on the planet as emotional as money. So now there is a demand for 220 million dollars to be redeemed on immediate request. They want all their investments redeemed. They want all their shares returned. I have a week to find 200 million dollars. If I'm lucky.

There is one place I can go to. There is one person I can talk to. This is the only reason I would ever come back here.

The woman on reception smiles with the kind of calm confidence you only really get when your Mandarin is as fluent as hers and your hair is as blonde as hers and your clothes are as crisp as hers and your skin is as soft and as clear.

She has no computer on her desk. There is only one computer in this whole building with the capacity to send and to receive emails. She has a ledger. She has a diary. She writes with the most beautiful pen I've ever seen. She smiles the smile of a thousand years. She brings me a coffee and an iced glacial mineral water and touches my arm ever so gently and tells me he's ready and asks me to step inside.

He looks up from his desk and he stands and comes to hold me.
He smells absolutely fantastic.
His skin looks just beautiful.
He's not changed since the days in the academy.
He's not changed since we were ski-ing together.
He's not changed since we went sailing together.
He's not changed since we were eighteen years old.
His face has frozen still into time.

He says 'hello' to me more directly than anybody has said 'hello' to me before.
He says 'hello' to me as though he's looking into my soul.

He asks me how I've been. He asks me how my wife is. He asks me how my son is. He tells me about his child. He tells me about his wife. He asks me what I'm doing tonight. His family have a box in the opera house. His family paid for a box in the opera house. His family paid for a wing of the opera house. They've had a box in the opera house for 126 years. Would I like to take his box in the opera house tonight?

He enjoys my shirt. He enjoys my smell too he said.

'So. Escamillo,' he says to me. 'How can I help you?'

I ask him if he's ever thought about the future of beef consumption in China.

His smile is as calm as a lake. He looks into my eyes. For a second I think that he knows. Does he know? He can't possibly know.

I can't tell you how I know.
You just have to trust me.
You've trusted me before.

I get through today and I'm fine.
If I get through today I could fly. If I could get through today I will never die.
If I get through today you would not believe the amount of money I will make for you and for your family.

I look so deeply into his eyes I can see the backs of his retina.
I wait.
He smiles.
He trusts me.

He takes me into, there's an office in the room next door to his.
And in this office next door is a man I have known for twenty years.
He is the cashier.
He smiles at me when my situation is explained.
His smile is a smile of warmth and reason.
He tells me he doesn't need my passport number.
He tells me he doesn't need my account details.
He doesn't need information from me at all. He grins at me.

He types twenty-five numbers into the only computer in the whole building. He makes one phone call and everything is completed with immediate effect. The money is transferred with immediate effect. All of a sudden everything in the universe is lighter than it has ever been.

Even the greatest stars
Discover themselves in the looking glass

Chorus   We hear police going door to door
We hear you tell us to stay inside
We hear that the weather is turning strange
We hear the televisions on downstairs
We hear him say he can't love her now
We hear the thump of lead in the alley
We hear the scratch of rats at the window
We hear the camcorder starting to hum

The Singer   I leave the rehearsals after the first day. I can't for the life of me remember the address of my apartment. I have to look in my emails to find it again.

I can't remember my email password at first but then I do and I have fifteen new emails. I'm looking at the names of the people who'd written them. I can't remember who half of them are.

It feels for a very short time like I can't remember anything. It feels like I can't remember who the other people in my family were or what the name of the town I was born in was.

I decide to call my boyfriend. I decide to ask him. I haven't spoken to him for weeks and weeks and weeks. It's the middle of the night where he is. That doesn't matter. He never minds about things like that.

Carmen   My dad wanted me to be a cellist. He made me play for him. Every time I dropped a note he'd hit the back of my head with this little piece of wood he kept. Like bigger than a ruler. He never hit me hard. But it was repetitive. It never stopped.

I only ever listen to techno nowadays.

I'm glad he's dead.

The Singer   I keep seeing the same four people. I see them everywhere.

There's a moment when I realise exactly who they are. It's Carmen, the lover. And Don José, the fighter. And Micaëla, the lost girl. And Escamillo.

Don José   The hotel at the station is glorious. We spent a night there one time. My second husband and I. This was years ago. Years before he died. Shortly after I came here with him. Shortly after I left you.

The bed was huge and comfortable. It had the most deep and comfortable pillows I've ever slept on. We lay in bed for hours as the morning rose. We held each other. I remember the feeling of his skin.

My stomach quivered as he kissed me. I didn't bite my tongue. I didn't try and stay quiet. My lungs filled with such love for him. You two were probably at school at the time. You were probably doing your homework or something.

In the Chinese quarter behind the railway the smell of herbs cooking suddenly bursts into the air. And of duck frying. And of chicken grilling.

I go to the place where I always go. I sit at the table I always sit at. They don't mind that I don't order food. They bring me my tea. A song plays on the radio.

Carmen   I have my own key. I let myself in. Call out. Mum. Mum. Mother. Hey, Mum, you deaf bitch where the fuck are you?

Don José   Golden days before they end,
Whisper secrets to the wind
Your baby won't be near you anymore.

Tender nights before they fly
And falling stars that seem to cry
Your baby doesn't want you anymore.

Carmen   She's in her room. She's sleeping. I sit on the bed. I look at her. Her breathing is unbelievably slow. I've never seen another living animal breathe as slowly as her. It's like –

Don José   You will never know how your father cried when I told him that I had decided to leave him. I stood there looking at him crying and didn't feel anything at all. Not anger or pity or sadness or contempt. It was like looking at an odd piece of furniture.

Carmen   I watch her.

I sing to her.

Love is like a rebellious bird.

Don José   You will never know how when my second husband was dying he was in such terrible pain. He lay on his back really properly screaming, howling that it hurt, it hurt, it hurt, it hurt. I looked at the doctor. I asked him why this was happening. He looked confused, as though he couldn't remember what the word 'why' meant any more.

Carmen   She's slept in this room for thirty-five years. Every night.

Don José   If I wear my coat it will get warm.
If I light another cigarette the bus will come.
If I leave the table to go out for a cigarette you will be here when I come back.

Carmen   There's a pillow on the other side of her bed. My dad's pillow. I pick it up. I smell it. I think for a second I can smell him on it. I can't.

Don José   Where do you think you go when you die? What's your favourite ice cream? When you dance where do you look with your eyes? What did you do on your twenty-first birthday? When you walk what do you do with your hands? When you have sex do you kiss with your eyes open or closed? Who is your best friend? Where do you most wish you could live? What do you look like when you sleep?

Carmen   She wakes up. She looks confused. She looks at me. She recoils. I smile at her. It's me, Carmen.

I go into her bathroom. I find some lotion. I clean myself. I piss. I brush my teeth with her toothbrush. I stare at my teeth in the mirror. I go into her kitchen. I make her some coffee. I take it to her. I'm tempted to pour it on her face. I decide not to.

I put it down. I give her a kiss goodbye. Tell her I'll see her next week. I leave.

Don José   I will tell you that I love you.

Carmen   The train on the way back into town is much busier than it was on the way out and when I sit down there's some fucking pregnant woman shoving her fucking baby in my face.

I get out of the station and this other woman, this fucking stupid fucking woman gets out of her taxi that she's driving for some reason and heads towards me to go into the station and just nearly fucking walks right into me because she just isn't looking where she's going.

Don José   I won't tell you how I stood outside the cafe watching you for ten minutes before I came in and how I had to catch my breath.

The Singer   I'm fine. I am. You know? Really. Everything's fine. The intendant's fine and the director's fine and the conductor's fine and the ensemble's fine and the children are, all of them fine.

They tell me where to stand. And how to move my arms. And what dress to wear. And how to come onto the stage. They tell me when to look at *him* and when to look at *him* and what to wear when I look at him and where to put my hands when I look at him. And they never, ever, never tell me who the fuck I am meant to be. That I have to decide upon for myself.

And in the last rehearsal Don José gets a hard-on in the prison scene. I'm so excited.

He sings the flower song. I whisper into his ear. 'Bravo.'

Carmen   There's a hotel by the side of the railway where the rooms cost 30 euros and there is never any staff, ever.

People don't actually work in these hotels anymore. You book your room online and pay for it online. Put your credit card in a fucking box when you get there. It punches out your room key.

I sit at the bar.

I buy a gin and tonic. The barman never once looks me in the eyes.

He is quite shockingly beautiful.

He's about twenty-three years old.

His skin looks like its made out of silk.

I check my Twitter feed.

I check my timeline.

I update my status.

I check my tumblr.

I check my emails. Delete three of them.

I check my Vine account.

I search for myself on Twitter.

There are twelve other people with my name ahead of me.

Nobody is talking about me.

I check out Tinder.

I check out Grindr.

I finish my drink.

Piss. Wash my hands. Try to wash the smell of his cologne off my hands. I can't. It's on the collar of my new shirt. I catch it. I gag a bit.

As I leave the hotel I catch the bartender's eye. Wink at him. He likes that. It's the little touches.

Postcards have started to appear in phone boxes again. Like in the nineties. That must mean something about people getting poorer or people getting richer or something. Boys waxed up, donning a quirky hat and a phone number.

I know three boys who have died in this work in the past eighteen months. Part of it's carelessness. Some of it's self-inflicted.

I step out of the hotel and there, right in front of the hotel door, a motorbike has crashed into the side of the bridge. I didn't notice it before I came in. It must have happened while I was in there. I didn't hear anything. There are cops everywhere. Most of them smiling. Laughing a bit. Talking on their walkie talkies. A body lies in the middle of the road.

Its limbs are skewed at the weirdest angle. A girl stands at the side of the road talking to one of the policemen. She's fucking about twelve years old. She sees me looking at her. She looks away. She looks back. Of course she does.

The Singer   Last week, out of the blue, the intendant asks me to come into his room.

Tell me. Do you like it here? Do you like this house? Do you like me? Would you like to work here again? Would you like to work for me again?
Well maybe you should start acting like you do. Maybe you should show a bit of respect around here. Maybe you should stop wandering round with your eyes made of glass all the time, huh? Maybe you should do a day's work for once in your life.

Are you crying?
Don't cry.
It's really annoying. Watching you cry.
Ha!
I'll call your manager.
Tell him you were crying.
See how much he thinks you're worth then, eh?

Do you know who I am? Have you got the slightest idea who the fuck I am?

I don't have the heart to tell him that I'm not really sure anymore. I can't really remember. I'm tempted to look it up on my phone.

Micaëla   Alexander left me after I asked him what kind of porn he liked and what were his favourite films and I went and found the same films on Pornhub and watched them myself and got off on them a bit and when I told him he said I'd violated his privacy and he felt exposed and called me weird and said I'd betrayed him.

That, to me, is just downright stupid.

I only really met him for the first time when we Skyped each other. Well that's not actually true. We'd met each other before. Clearly. But not really met each other. Not actually talked. I Skyped him to talk about an essay because I missed a tutorial. When I was talking to him I took my bra off in the middle of our conversation. I have no idea why I did that. He didn't know what to say. I asked him if he wanted to see my tits and he said that he did and so I took my T-shirt off we did do a bit of wanking and he is sixty-three and married so I felt guilty even though it was just Skype.

But that was our first date, in a way. So to complain about me violating him through the computer given that this whole thing started on a computer seems just absurd to me.

Sometimes I go on Twitter and tell people we're getting married. Sometimes I go on Facebook and talk about sexual encounters that we've had even though they're made up. I love that feeling. I feel very alive.

I turned a corner into the square behind the cathedral at the north side of the bridges and the entire place was empty. All of a sudden everybody had disappeared. The air became still. I must have been walking over other people's graves. Centuries and centuries of graves.

I found myself thinking about him so much that I couldn't walk straight. The sun was burning my head so I went into the toilets of the cathedral cafe and put my hand in my pants and remembered the last time we spoke and the things that he said to me and the things that he showed me and the feeling of the chairs in his office and the smell of his shirts and the way he made me feel and stayed there for five minutes.

When I come out of the cathedral there's a man in a beautiful suit staring into his phone and he doesn't notice me. He nearly walks into me. He doesn't.

Alexander left me because I told him I loved him and boys find that a very difficult thing to get their heads around.

The last time we spoke before I Skyped him, at the end of our tutorial Alexander said that I was looking glum. I'm not. I said. I did my biggest smile. Are you one of those people? He asked me. Who people think of as being in a bad mood when they're not in a bad mood? Are you one of those people that never says anything when other people want them to.

It's just that I never have much to say. So I keep quiet.

He is the only person who has ever noticed that I find saying things hard. What effect did he expect that to have on me, precisely? What did he fucking think would happen?

I headed towards the river.

'The eternal sunshine of the spotless mind
Each prayer accepted and each wish resigned'

I sent him photographs of myself. I found the perfect way of taking a photograph of myself with my fingers inside me.

There is nothing more vulnerable that you can do to another human than to photograph yourself like that. It is the most honest thing you can do.

I always said I wanted the memories without the photographs but I realise now that memory doesn't mean anything. Memories are lies. A photograph is an honest and objective record of the things that have happened.

I thought about this as I watched tourists taking photographs of the cathedral from the river. What is the point of a photograph of a cathedral? It's so that in the future we can remember that once upon a time we were alive.

I crossed the river with my shitty little essay stuffed into my backpack and it felt like instead of an essay I was carrying a weight in there. It was a weight of sadness so profound that it might simply be lighter for everybody I loved if I didn't exist any more. Not better. Not more exciting. Just lighter. The world would be lighter if I wasn't in it.

That was when I thought about the water.

Chorus   We taste the black coffee on our lips.
We taste the salt in our sweat these days.
We taste the sad chaos of time zones.
We taste the sugar in the apple juice.
We taste the cream on our silver spoons.
We taste the colours on your You Tube films.
We taste the architecture in the street.
We taste your skin in between our teeth.

The Singer   My boyfriend sounds like the crackle of
burning wood.
My boyfriend smells of leather and tangerine.
My boyfriend tastes of ice cream and coffee and cigarettes.
My boyfriend feels like the soft hair on a horse's hide.
My boyfriend is the colour of the sunrise in the countryside.

Don José   There's something I want to tell you about. It's
something I very much want to describe.

Escamillo   The transfer has been made. My whole world
has been saved. It makes me vertiginous.
I've got four hours before I need to go back to the hotel. I
have a flight first thing tomorrow morning.

Don José   You arrived when you promised you would. You
looked stunning to me. Your jeans were new and your
T-shirt was crisp and bright, bright yellow and your eyes,
when you took your sunglasses off, it was like they were the
greenest eyes that I had ever seen.

Escamillo   I decide I'm going to go for a walk.

I know exactly where I'm going to go.

Don José   I know that we talked for hours and I liked to
listen to you talk. It's funny because your voice was odd to
me and I liked its oddness. But every so often there would
be a vowel sound or a consonant sound or an utterance that
you would make that would sting me and sing like a shock in
my veins because there was something of other voices that I
knew in your voice and that was a miracle.

Escamillo   The sun sparkles off the matt grey brick and the matt grey stone and the beautifully designed latticework and the chrome of the railway station. Everything here in fact is matt grey. People sit in matt grey suits and matt grey skirts and drink cold, cold champagne.

They face the future with an unswerving certainty. Nobody here knows the slightest possibility of doubt.

And then one day. As if by magic.

Don José   Deoxyribonucleic acid.

Escamillo   I head away from the financial district and move up to the north.

I've not walked like this for years and years and years.

Don José   I listened to you talk to me about your sister and your father and how everything went with your exams. And about your work and the people you work with and the things that you do and how well you do them. And the music that you like and the films that you like and the television you like and the books that you like and the websites that you like and the food that you like and the places that you like.

Escamillo   The more that I walk the redder everything seems to become.

Don José   I started to talking to you about driving for a while and then realised that I really didn't know what to say about it.

Escamillo   The houses around here have beautiful original artwork and well-filled fruit bowls. I always hated that.

There was a man who lived down the road from here who used to throw plastic bags full of shit into his neighbour's back gardens. I think about him for a while. Of all the people I met here I seem to miss him most.

Don José   It was when I was talking to you about my life. I was talking to you about the people I'd worked with and

about all the places that I've been to. These places are
nowhere nearly as exciting as the places you've been to. I felt
a bit embarrassed talking about them in fact but, it was then,
when I was talking, right then, you leant forward and
without saying anything you picked up the teapot and you
poured me more tea and you put in some sugar and the
sugar you put in was the exact right amount. It was like, in
that moment, you'd noticed me. It was like in that moment
there was proof that you'd watched me and looked at me
and thought about me and learnt how I drank my tea.

Escamillo   And then, finally, as though almost unaware of
it, I happen to walk down the street where I first met my
wife. On this street is the house where we first fucked. And
the room where my son was first born.

Don José   I had to try my hardest to stop myself from
crying.
I had to try my hardest to stop myself from breaking down
and kissing you again and again and again and again.
I had to try my hardest to stop myself from laughing
out loud.
I had to stop myself from grabbing your wrist where you
held the teapot and holding on as tight as I can and never,
not ever, never letting go.

Escamillo   The houses here are much smaller than I
remember.

And I find to my astonishment I can't really remember
which number it was.

The most important house I have ever known. I can't
remember what number it was any more.

Don José   When I first came to this country it was the first
time I'd ever seen snow. This was before I met your father. I
couldn't believe my eyes. It looked like giant marshmallow
butterflies floating around in the sky and I stood and I
watched it fall. I let it fall onto my face.

I'd never seen an ocean before he took me to see it.
I had no idea that anything could be as big as that.

Would you like to see me again?
Maybe every so often?

Escamillo   I should call her. I should tell her where I am.
I should take a photograph of where I am and send it home
to her.

Don José   When you left we kissed each other goodbye on
the cheek. I held your arm longer than you held mine. Our
cheeks kind of bashed into each other so it was more like we
were rubbing chins than actually kissing one another.

I wanted to ask you what deodorant you were wearing so I
could go and buy a can of it and spray it onto my clothes on
days when I was feeling sad.

I gave you my number.

I didn't give any message to give to your sister because I
thought that would have been rude.

I watched you walk away until you got right around the
corner. I felt like running after you to watch you walk into
the station and onto your train but I didn't.

I left the cafe. I left the station area. I drove.

The Singer   It takes him a bit longer to answer the phone
than I'd have thought. The ringing tone is strange. It's a
different ringing tone to the one it normally is when I ring
him at home. He answers the phone after a while though.
He sounds really tired. The line's terrible. His voice sounds
like it's coming from a long way away. He doesn't say my
name. My name can't have come up on the caller ID on his
phone. He answers as though he was talking to a total
stranger.

Hello? Hello who is this?

I tell him that it's me. I tell him I'm sorry for calling so late. I
just need to talk to him. Something's happened. I want to
tell him about it. It's like he can't even hear me.

Hello? Hello? Is anybody there? Can you hear me? I'm sorry. I can't hear you. I can't hear anything. I'm going to go okay? I'm going to go now.

He hangs up. I call back. It goes straight to his answer machine. I don't leave a message.

Micaëla   Alexander left me because he told me I was too young to have a long-term relationship and nyway I would probably end up leaving town or going back home when I graduated. He wasn't sure if he wanted to leave this place.

He told me that everything we'd shared together had kind of been him doing me a favour. He had bestowed his honour upon me. I should be grateful because it kind of had helped me out a bit because my work had started off pretty good but over the past few months had become really quite mediocre. He'd argued my corner in the senior common room and largely he'd won the arguments.

He just wanted a bit of fun. He just wanted the occasional wank. It wasn't that different from pornography. It wasn't that different from a webcam. It was cheaper than a webcam. I wasn't as experienced as some of the other girls he'd spoken to on webcams.

I have the capacity to recall every word of that last conversation. When I recall it I can see it written down in my head like a kind of script. I was reading this script as I was passing the train station on the way to the campus office and so although I really was looking in the direction of the motorbike as it accelerated into the bridge that the trains run on, and smashed into the foot of that bridge and the boy on the motorbike flew, I mean really flew, through the air in the direction he'd been going but the bike had stopped and so he'd landed on his shoulder and bounced and then landed on his back and then lay there still as a leather sack full of bones and didn't make a sound. Although I saw all that I didn't really understand what I was looking at.

I should have been able to watch it on repeat. I should have been able to slow it down or pause it. I couldn't.

He lay quite still. The traffic stopped. All the car horns sang out like a horrible choir. A boy standing outside a hotel bar stared at me for what felt like ages.

The police didn't understand what I meant when I said that I'd seen everything but in a way I just didn't see anything.

They thought I was lying. They thought I was taking the piss out of them.

One of them even asked me if I was taking the piss out of him.

Yes, officer. I saw everything. I saw all of it.
I didn't really see it at all.

One of the police officers asked me if I needed a taxi to take me where I was going and he flagged one for me before I could answer. The driver looked really confused when I told her I didn't have any money. She asked me what I stopped her for.

Alexander left me because I told him I didn't fancy him anymore.

That was about the closest thing I ever came to telling him the truth. I don't think he heard me. I think he was looking at the image of himself in the little window at the bottom of the screen.

I focused on the stripy T-shirt that he was wearing and how stupid and fat and idiotic he looked in it when I left my essay in the faculty office and signed my submission paper and walked away.

My brain was still kind of thinking about how still the boy on the motorbike had been.

I don't think I've ever seen a human being as still as that ever in my whole life.

Once I was driving at night with my father late at night to my grandmother's house in the country when out of nowhere this baby deer leapt from the side of the road and my dad hit it.

We got out. It was lying yards in front of us in the road. It was panting very heavily and in the night-time under the car headlights it looked kind of fantastic. Its eyes were shining. It was looking straight at me. I looked straight back deep into these shining black eyes. There was a moment when the sparkle in the eyes just disappeared completely. It stopped breathing. We dragged it to the side of the road. We drove on to see my grandmother.

Crossing back over the river I saw the strangest thing. A group of women had all gathered together at the edge of the water and they were going for a fucking swim in it. I wanted to shout out to ask them what the fuck they thought they were doing. They looked completely beautiful.

One of them, she had black hair, thick black hair rolling down to her waist and she looked like she was Spanish or that she was a gipsy or something. She was singing. I couldn't hear what she was singing because of the noise of the traffic but I watched her sing and my heart filled up.

Chorus   We feel the ice in the gasoline.
We feel the wind down our vertebrae.
We feel the stones in our ankle bones.
We feel the hair on our necks stand up.
We feel the press of your forearm skin.
We feel the skin of your telephone.
We feel the heat of your coffee cup.
We feel the sand in your dinner plate.

The Singer   The traffic outside the stage entrance tonight is brought to a to a standstill and for a while I can't figure out why. For a while I think it's for me. Did I do this? Are these people trying to see me? I get closer. I see what's happened.

A nineteen-year-old boy has his motorcycle helmet removed and his head is rested against the side of the pavement.

He's entirely motionless. He's dead.

Carmen   Tonight there's an opera playing in town. The huge old chocolate box opera house by the river. I saw a poster for it. My namesake.

The Singer   For a moment I can't remember the way from the stage door to the canteen. I can't remember the name of the woman in the canteen. I can't remember the way from the canteen to my dressing room or from my dressing room to the stage. I can't remember where I'm meant to stand. I can't remember my words. I can't remember how the tune goes. I can't remember the name of my character. Should I look it up on my phone? I bet I could find it there somewhere.

I can't stop thinking about the boy.

Escamillo   Proprioception is the sense that we have of our relationship to our own bodies in the world. It's how we know when we fall over to move our head so that our eyes line up with the horizon.

Micaëla   Alexander left me because I told him I wanted his baby and I was kind of joking and I was kind of not joking.

Don José   The traffic on the south side of the river has slowed down to a crawl. Something's happened. I can't tell what it is. Some stupid-looking girl stops me. She's surrounded by police officers. She asks me if I could give her a ride for free. The police all watch to see my reaction. I drive away.

Carmen   I like an Opera audience. You can make a good bit of money from an opera audience. They pour out from their fantasy all flushed with romance and a sense of their own wealth. All you have to do is look cute. Smile at them.

The Singer   I make my way to my dressing room eventually. My dresser's waiting for me.

She sits outside my room. All the time. Waiting for the tiniest noise. Standing to attention at the slightest noise. Getting ready. Poised. Always.

Is it her voice? Has it been her all along?

Don José   I find out what had happened on the radio. There's been an accident. A motorcyclist was killed. He was nineteen. He was the one who fucked all the traffic up.

Micaëla   I think Alexander would be a good dad even though he'd probably die when the baby was really young but in a sense that would be fine and probably quite good and in a way quite romantic.

Escamillo   It was then. Coming out of that crowd. Just then. That I saw her for the first time.

Micaëla   Death's good for babies. That's what death's for. We die so that we can make more room. That's the whole point.

I shouldn't be sad about people dying. I should be happy. In a way, when somebody dies it's quite exciting. Death is a time for something new to start. I want to ring my grandmother's funeral and tell everybody there to think about all the things they can do now. They should think about all the ways their life has changed and all the new things that might happen now and the freedom they might have and the way there is less now between them and the whole sky.

Carmen   There's a handful of cafes just by the opera house where they sell beautiful coffee in gorgeous bone-china cups. There's a good view of the river. You can watch the audience arrive and show yourself like you're in a shop window. I have a good hard think about my plans for the night. I decide to head there and to see what I can see.

Don José   I spend a small amount of time thinking about my own death. It just seems impossible to me. After a life so amazingly normal.

Escamillo   She came out of the grocery store ahead of me and we shared eye contact for about half a second. It felt like I'd never seen anything.

Don José   You get up. You have a day. Do a job. And do another day. Have some food. Then die. Fucking actually die.

The Singer   I have my flower. I check. I have my ring. I check. I've got everything in order.

I keep thinking about the dead boy's skin. I keep thinking about the dead boy's bones. I can't figure out what the point of a body is when the life inside it has disappeared. It's redundant now.

Escamillo   I have no idea who she was. It felt like I'd known her all my life. I had no idea where she came from or where she was going. I have absolutely no idea how old she is. It felt like I was waiting for this to happen.

She was strong and soft and her skin looked like milk and her hair bobbed like a soft rope of honey as she turned and walked away from me.

Her bag bouncing on her back as she drank from a bottle of coke and read emails on her phone kind of caught me completely by surprise.

I followed her.

Micaëla   I call my dad. I want to tell him. Dad – Dad – Dad – It's me.

I can't get through. I get the answer machine message.

It's me. Call me.

I tweet about my grandmother.

I tweet about the river.

I wonder if he'll have collected my essay yet. I wonder if he'll read mine first.

Carmen   Outside the theatre there's a couple. She's got her hands wrapped around his neck. She's kissing him full on the mouth. At the very moment I'm passing her she stops. Pulls away. Looks at him. Rests her nose on his chin.

Her face is so happy that it looks like a miracle.

The thing is to me, that matters. This isn't about money. This isn't about the colour of my skin. It's not about politics. I don't give a fuck about politics. I hear people talk about politics and my eyes glaze over. You can stick your politics up your cock. This is about the look in her eyes and the love in his heart and the way that we make each other feel.

The Singer   Tonight. It's going to be a big night. Tonight they want their go-go dancer. Tonight they want a lap dance. Tonight they want their porn star.

Escamillo   Have you ever done this? Have you ever done this to anybody? Have you ever followed somebody? They don't know. They have no idea what you're doing. It's a city. We're living in a city. If she'd turned and asked me what I was doing I would have looked at her like she was insane.

She turned off the main road and into a circus of terraced houses. I thought she was going to go into a house there. Please God don't go into one of the houses here. She didn't. She walked out of the circus and back onto a side street. I swear in the sunshine her hair almost burned. I swear in the sunshine the streets started to melt. I swear there was sweat and it was pouring down the small of my back. I had nothing to drink. I needed a drink.

Would you like to come for a drink with me?
Who are you?
I'm sorry I was just noticing you. I was watching you. I wondered if you wanted to come for a drink with me?

I don't say anything to her. Not out loud. Not so she could hear it. I start to lose a little bit of sense of what I'm actually saying out loud and what is just being said inside my skull.

I have seventeen unread emails on my iPhone.
I have five missed calls.
I have three text messages.
I can reply to them now.
The money has been transferred with immediate effect.
Nothing. Will. Ever. Be a problem. Ever. Again.

She stops to cross at a junction of a main road. I can't stop twenty yards behind her. I can't just stand still in the middle of the road.

I walk up to the junction.

I stand an inch away from her.

She's wearing a red Helmut Lang cap sleeved dress.

I lift my hand to scratch my cheek and blood gushed all the way inside me. I feel its gush like a bucket of water. As I lift my hand I grace the back of her hair and I feel monumentally alive.

The lights change.

She crosses the road.

I can't move. I stop.

I watch her.

I turn.

I walk away.

And just at that moment my bones turn to liquid. I have no idea how I manage to stay standing on my feet. I try as hard as I can to think about my wife's face.

I love my wife with all my soul.

I take out my phone. I'm determined to text my wife but I catch my reflection on the black mirror of my turned off phone and for a second I can't recognise my face.

Every single email in my inbox is from the girl in the red Helmut Lang dress. I don't know how she got my address. I don't even know her name.

She's writing to me to tell me she knows I've been following her. She's writing to me to tell me she's been waiting for me all of her life. She's writing to tell me how young she is. She's writing to me to check that I landed safely. She emails me five times to ask about the meeting. She writes to me to tell me that she knows the money will be lost. She knows there is no way I could ever pay it back. She writes to me to tell me she knows so much more about beef consumption in China.

I look up. I look around. She's gone. She's completely disappeared.

Where is she? Where's she gone to? Hello? Where are you? Where have you gone?

I shudder into focus outside the cathedral. I nearly walk right into some stupid student or something, some girl. She looks flustered. She's not paying the slightest bit of attention to where she's going. She comes out of the cathedral exit. Her cheeks are all flushed. I'm on the north side of the river. I have absolutely no idea how I made it this far.

It's low tide on the river and it's graced by the sunshine. And on the south bank, I think, is it me? Is it me or is there a group of women in the water there? Washing their clothes? It's like they're singing? Are they singing? Are those women singing?

Holidaymakers tossing water bottles up in the air shine in the sunshine.
Secretaries with their fat calves wobbling over the bridge shine in the sunshine.
Investment bankers smoking cigars of certainty, confident of the fearless success of their recovery from catastrophe shine

in the sunshine
And the church spire shines in the sunshine.
And the opera singer hiding behind reflective sunglasses
shines in the sunshine.
And the teenage girl looking for a moment deep into the
belly of the dirt brown smear of the water shines in the
sunshine.
And a young boy in a beautiful shirt tries to stop himself
from crying as he shines in the sunshine.
And a taxi driver slides her car into second gear as she shines
in the sunshine.
And the buses
And the bicycles
And the commuters
And everything
And Europe crumbling
Defiant
Shines in the sunshine.

And as I realise this I step into the road.
I don't stop to look if any cars are coming.
I don't stop to see if any buses are coming.
I think about the way a red Helmut Lang dress might fall to
the floor of my hotel room.
I think about his look in his eyes when he talked about his
wife and his son and the ski-ing holiday and how much he
remembers my mother and tells me that he won't need my
passport number and that the money will be transferred
with immediate effect.
I remember the smell of my wife.
I don't give a shit about the motorbike as it swerves to
avoid me.

The Singer   I wonder how it would feel to have somebody
carefully place my head on the side of the sidewalk like that.
I wonder how it would feel as they remove my helmet. I
wonder what their faces would be like as they look in horror

at the crack at the back of my skull. I wonder about how it would be to feel that stillness.

Don José   A man gets into my car and asks me to take him to the opera. He's dressed beautifully but he has a thin skin of sweat soaking his face. I don't even need to think about my route. So my brain drifts.

The Singer   When I move my hands she seems to move her hands too.
When I raise my arms her arms raise too.
When I sing she sings at exactly the same time in exactly the same way.
When I think she thinks exactly the same thoughts.
And now I'm not sure if the thoughts are my thoughts at all.
Or if the voice is my voice.
Or the arms and hands are mine or if all of these things belong to Carmen.

Carmen   I order an espresso to shake out the taste of cheap gin. It tastes horrible.

I look up. The boy from the hotel bar is sitting at another table reading his iPhone. I stare at him. He looks up from his phone. He stares straight at me. I smile at him. He half smiles back. I can't believe he's here. How did he get here so quickly?

It's not him. It looks like him. It's not.

I go up to him anyway. I sit at his table. He looks up. Says hi with a look of total confusion on his face. He's a lot older than I thought he was.

Hi.

There are fossils on the side of the river. Dinosaur bones. You can find them. Did you know that?

Can you understand me? Can you understand what language I'm speaking in?

I see the look in his eyes. I made him look like that.

He stands up and walks away. Don't go. What? Stay for a bit. What? Please. As he's walking away I watch him and as I watch him I notice that he has absolutely no arse.

The Singer   The conductor looks at me with suspicion in his eyes. He knows what I'm going to do. The director looks at me with terror in her eyes. She knows what I'm going to do. The intendant comes into my room and places a hand gently on my shoulder. He knows. The children in the ensemble know. My dresser knows. The way the make-up girl runs her fingers through my hair. She knows. The smell of her skin cream. She's been here for hours and hours and hours. The head on my pillow. Those people I keep seeing. I see them everywhere. The voice in my head. They know.

Don José   I know exactly what I'm going to do. There's part of me thinks it's not even a decision. I am going to follow you for the rest of your life. There's part of me knows I will climb mountains for you. I will live in the desert for you. I will watch your life unfold and never speak to you ever again, ever. I will murder you and stay with your dead body in the afternoon in the sunshine.

Chorus   Think of a word
The worst word you could possibly think of
Think of another word
Put them together
Search

The Singer   Don't stop me. Don't stop me. If you try and stop me I'll cut out your heart.

Micaëla   My dad rang me back. I missed his call. I think my phone was on silent. He left a message. I listen to it. I listen to it again to hear the sound of his voice. I listen to it for a third time. I listen to it again.

The Singer   Do you smile because you're happy or feel happy because you smile?
Do you kill because you feel angry or feel angry because you kill?

Do you fuck because you feel horny or feel horny because you fuck?

Am I doing this because I feel scared or do I feel scared because I'm doing this?

Escamillo   Do I have a nosebleed? Have I got blood on my face? Do I smell strange? Have I got shit on my shoe? As I came back out of my hotel and took the taxi to the opera and showed my ticket to the usher and asked directions to my box and made my way to my box everybody looked at me as though I was really strange.

Does everybody in this whole room realise what I've done?

The Singer   I can hear them. *Ces gens là*. They know I'm listening to them. They know I'm waiting. I stare into her eyes in the little black mirror on my phone. Sweet sweet sweet sweet Carmen.

Escamillo   I've not eaten all day.

I've drunk five litres of water.

I've not had a conversation with a living person since this morning. The seats in the opera are soft and red and velvet and lush and gorgeous and deep and warm.

I like the sound that the orchestra plays as they find their note.

I like the way the audience quietens.

I like the way the music starts.

I know this music. Deep inside my bones I know this music very well.

The Singer   I stand up.

Escamillo   I've heard this music all my life. I've heard this music as I've waited on hold for theatre tickets and for travel information and for holiday information and for banking information all my life.

The Singer   I gather my breath. I walk out of my room. I know exactly where I'm going to go. The voice in my head tells me exactly where to go.

Escamillo   *Toréador, en garde!, Toréador! Toréador!*
Et songe bien, oui, songe en combatant
Qu'un oeil noir te regarde
Et que l'amour t'attend
Toréador, L'amour, l'amour t'attend!

And then –

The Singer   My dresser looks at me.

Escamillo   And then –

The Singer   One moment. Just. I'll be one moment.

Escamillo   A note lasts for ever.

The Singer   I walk away from the stage area. I walk along the corridor. After a while she calls after me. Madam Carmen. We have to go. Madam Carmen. We have to go now.

Escamillo   Everybody is waiting for somebody to appear.

The whole room is waiting for somebody to appear.

Three thousand people are waiting for somebody to appear.

The note dies.

The Singer   The man on the stage entrance is reading a newspaper on his phone and it takes him a second after he buzzes me out to realise who I am and what I'm actually wearing.

Escamillo   A man in a suit walks to the front of the stage.

The Singer   And by the time he does I'm away.

Escamillo   He stares up at the ceiling. He smiles.

The Singer   I think that I hear somebody say something. Did somebody say something?

Escamillo   He's terribly, terribly sorry to say –

The Singer   I look behind me but

oh

oh

oh

there's absolutely nothing there.

Escamillo   Nobody knows what to say to one another so everybody talks to one another in a way that we would never have talked to one another before. These are the first conversations I've had all afternoon. I'm not quite sure if my jaw is working right. Nobody seems to notice.

The Singer   When I try to remember where I've come from I realise there's nothing there.

Escamillo   We are given clear and simple instructions about how we can apply online to have our money refunded.

The Singer   I try to think about my dressing room but I realise there's nothing there. In the front of house there's nothing there. In the bars and the cloakrooms there's nothing there. In the offices at the back of the building there's nothing there either

Escamillo   We walk out of the opera house. It's still light outside. None of us had expected that.

The Singer   I try to think about the stage set. I realise there's nothing there. Out there in the auditorium I realise there's nothing there. I look around me. The streets have disappeared. The buildings have disappeared. The river has disappeared. The train station has disappeared. Everything has disappeared. None of this is real.

Escamillo   I want to ask the people around me where they're going and what they're doing. Ask if it's okay if I join them.

The Singer   I try to look on my phone to find out what's happened but I can't turn it on. It won't turn on. I look into it. All I can see is my own reflection.

Escamillo   I go for a beer by a cafe at the side of the opera house and watch the sun fall on the water. It's like I can feel every last drop of the beer all over my tongue.

The Singer   A rank of taxis waits outside the opera house.

Three women leave the offices in the beautiful old building across the square from where I'm standing. They're smoking cigarettes and they link their arms together and they're singing. I can't hear the song that they're singing.

Two policemen stand on the corner of the square and watch the women. They try to say goodnight to them but the girls just start giggling. The policemen don't mind. They're used to this kind of thing.

Escamillo   After a while a boy comes and sits down at another table. He starts looking at me. He stands up. He comes towards me. Sits down right next to me. I think for a moment I've seen him before. I can't have seen him before. He's wearing a remarkable shirt. He says something to me. I can't understand what he's saying.

It's not that he's speaking a language I don't understand. He isn't.

It's not that I don't understand the individual words that he's using because I do. All of them.

It's that when he puts them in that order they don't make any sense to me at all.

I look at him.
I smile.
I finish my beer.
I walk away.

And suddenly as I walk it's like I've got hours more out of my life than I ever knew I had.

The beer tasted great.
The boys face as I walked away looked hilarious.
The music of the Opera singing interrupted in my head.
The night is alive.

I don't buy all the nonsense of people wanting to die to
escape from the agony of the world. I have no fucking time
for attempted suicides. There are so many attempted
suicides every fucking day that it is becoming boring for
ambulance drivers. It is just boring. These fuckers. With
their pathos and their ego. If you really want to die you are a
stupid cunt because it means you've not thought hard
enough about either how sparkling life can be or how final
and how shit and inexorable death is. You're flirting with
something fucking stupid. Which means you're fucking
stupid and that handful of pills is just a waste of time for
somebody who could be curing a cancer patient or helping
somebody with a broken leg.

My Mother's here. Somewhere in this city. I should call her.

I go to my iPad. I go to the page that I always go to.
I type in my User Name.
I search for Maria.
Hi Maria.
She smiles just slightly off the centre of the screen.

Maria. Will you do something for me?
Will you touch the camera? If I touch my screen of my
computer and you touch your camera at the same time.

Just now.

Thank you.

I'll count down from three.

Three. Two. One.

Don José   I buy a packet of fruit sweets. I eat more sweets
than any other adult of my age that I know.

Suddenly I find that I appear to be talking.

My mouth is opening and closing and I can feel the movement of my tongue and my teeth and the feeling of the pressure from my diaphragm and words actual words real living throbbing words seem to be coming out as though I have something to say. I don't know what I'm saying. I don't know how loud I'm talking or who I'm talking to but I know, in my blood that I am talking and talking and talking and talking.

Chorus   We imagine a world without oxygen.
We imagine a world without food.
We imagine a world without nature.
We imagine a world without sugar.
We imagine a world without water.
We imagine a world without money.

Give us your hand. We'll read your palm.

Carmen   The night falls. It's ten o'clock. There's no movement from out of the Opera House so I go to have a closer look. I get there. I look in through the glass doors of the box office. There's nobody around. There's nobody there. The lights have been turned off. I didn't notice them turn the lights off. I didn't notice them lock the doors. When did that happen? When did everybody leave? When did everybody go home?

Excuse me? I'm sorry. Can you hear me? Is there anybody in there? Can anybody hear me? Is there anybody there?

The Singer   There's a moment when you speak a word and it takes flight.
Something which is just a shape becomes a sound.
Something which is just a shape becomes a gesture,
Something which is just a shape can smash somebody's heart into a million tiny pieces.
And then.
There's a moment. When you sing it.

Made in the USA
Columbia, SC
22 November 2024

47357450R00037